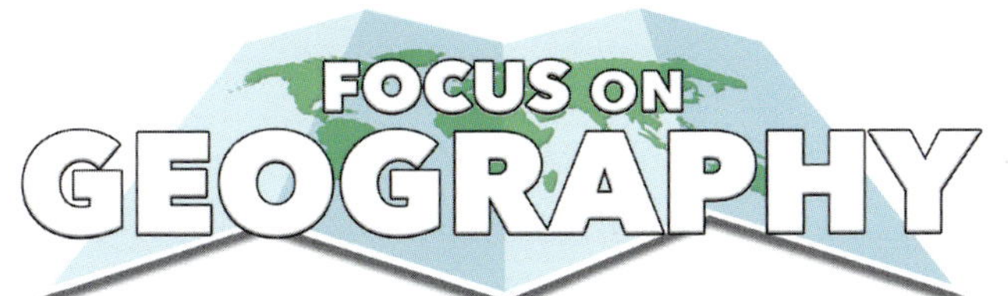

Focus on Pakistan

Ellen Rodger

A Crabtree Forest Book

Crabtree Publishing

crabtreebooks.com

Author: Ellen Rodger

Series research and development: Janine Deschenes

Editorial director: Kathy Middleton

Editor: Crystal Sikkens

Proofreader: Melissa Boyce

Design: Tammy McGarr

Print and production coordinator: Katherine Berti

IMAGE CREDITS

Shutterstock: Dave Primov, cover (top left); Jimmy Tran, cover (top right); Aqib Yasin, TOC; gaborbasch, p 4; Asianet-Pakistan, p 5 (top), p 26; Magsi, p 27 (top), p 36 (bottom), p 37 (top), Asianet-Pakistan, p 42 (top); Aqib Yasin, p 43 (bottom); Homo Cosmicos, p 6; A M Syed, p 13 (bottom), p 24 (top), p 41 (both images), p 42 (bottom), p 42 (bottom); Aleem Zahid Khan, p 14 (top); Dave Primov, p 15 (bottom); SkycopterFilms Archives, p 15 (top); Nova Photo Works, p 16 (top); gary yim, p 24 (bottom); Amir Mukhtar, p 25 (bottom); Faraz Hyder Jafri, p 25 (top); SkycopterFilms Archives, p 27 (bottom); Habibullah Qureshi, p 29 (middle); MFAHEEM FAHEEM, p 29 (top); khlongwangchao, p 30; M Selcuk Oner, p 31 (top); Johnny110, p 31 (middle); AlafStudio, p 32 (right); Tea Talk, p 32 (bottom left); Juana Nunez, p 34 (middle); Dave Primov, p 35 (right); Pises Tungittipokai, p 35 (top); Maharani afifah, p 36 (top); UmairHaider, p 37 (bottom); Iqbal Akhtar Hussain, p 38 (top); A Rehman 786, p 39 (top); Reo_graphy, p 40 (top); Katja Tsvetkova, p 44 (top); A M Syed, p 45 (top)

Wikimedia Commons: Zachaboi, p 11 (bottom right); Trish Mayo, p 18 (top); Public Domain, p 19 (top), p 22 (top), p 23 (top); Onef9day, p 40 (bottom);

Crabtree Publishing

crabtreebooks.com **800-387-7650**

In Canada: We acknowledge the financial support of the Government of Canada through the Canada Book Fund for our publishing activities.

Hardcover 978-1-0398-0644-3
Paperback 978-1-0398-0670-2
Ebook (pdf) 978-1-0398-0696-2
Epub 978-1-0398-0723-5

Published in Canada
Crabtree Publishing
616 Welland Avenue
St. Catharines, Ontario
L2M 5V6

Published in the United States
Crabtree Publishing
347 Fifth Avenue
Suite 1402-145
New York, New York, 10016

Library and Archives Canada Cataloguing in Publication
Available at Library and Archives Canada

Library of Congress Cataloging-in-Publication Data
Available at the Library of Congress

Printed in the U.S.A./012023/CG20220815

Contents

Introduction

Snapshot of a Busy Bazaar

Anarkali **Bazaar** is a busy place. It's a lively market and historic city neighborhood in Lahore, Pakistan. Lahore is Pakistan's second-largest city. Here, old blends seamlessly with new. Tightly packed buildings with carved wooden windows sit next to busy market stalls. Stall owners make **fragrant** karahis, or curries, and naan flatbreads for hungry Lahoris. Tea makers called chai wallahs send runners to serve steaming cups of sweet and spicy chai to merchants and customers. Women and men in traditional **shalwar kameez** mix with crowds of others in jeans and sneakers. They wander down crumbling alleys to bargain for everything from wedding clothing to cricket bats and cell phones.

Located outside Lahore's **medieval** walled city, Anarkali is one of Pakistan's oldest market bazaars. Residential neighborhoods, an important historical museum, and several universities spread out within its area. Anarkali is a window into Pakistan's past. It is also a picture of the present and future of Pakistan.

Bazaars are a feature of almost every city, town, and larger village in Pakistan. Modern shopping malls are common in the bigger cities, but many people still prefer to shop and eat at bazaars.

Eid al-Fitr is an important celebration for many Pakistanis. Bazaar vendors sell new clothing to wear or give as gifts during Eid al-Fitr.

People-Filled Cities

With 11 million residents, Lahore is vibrant and buzzing with people. People pack into cars, buses, and **tuk tuks** to go about their business. You might see an entire family of four whizzing in and out of traffic on a tiny motorbike. The air, especially in the hot, moist summer, is thick with exhaust fumes, making it hard to breathe at times.

Jeweled with mosques and **minarets** and neighborhoods old and new, Pakistan's many large cities are **densely** populated and ever-growing. Pakistanis from smaller rural villages move to cities every day to go to school or find work. People are the country's most plentiful **resource**. Many sprawling cities have been built around historic sites. Some are close to rural areas and ancient archaeological treasures.

Located in the province of Punjab, Lahore was the center of several ancient empires. The Badshahi Mosque was built from 1671–73 for a **Mughal** emperor. It was the largest mosque in the world for over 300 years.

Broken in Two

Pakistan is a modern country located in South Asia. It was formed in 1947 when India, then a **colony** of Great Britain, was broken into two independent countries. This breakup was called partition. Pakistan's territory was brought together from the eastern and northwestern parts of **British India**. It included an area carved from part of the former Indian province of Bengal, near Burma. After a bitter war, this part left Pakistan and became the independent country of Bangladesh in 1971.

Partition was difficult and violent. It mapped out borders based on religion. That lead to millions of people fleeing to either Pakistan or India as refugees. Partition also led to border and territory wars between Pakistan and India. Some of these conflicts continue to this day.

Borders and Neighbors

Every day at 6 p.m., several crossings on the long border between Pakistan and India hold border-closing ceremonies. At the Wagah crossing near Lahore, flags are lowered and border guards in dress uniforms stomp and kick high. They then fiercely stare at each other before shaking hands and closing the gates. India isn't Pakistan's only neighbor. It is also bordered by Iran and Afghanistan to the north and China to the northeast. It is separated from Tajikistan in the north by a thin strip of land called the Wakhan Corridor. Pakistan's location is a crossroads of the ancient trade routes of Western, South, Central, and East Asia and the Middle East. As a result, Pakistan is home to a **diverse** population of people from many different ethnic groups.

Pakistan-India border-crossing events attract tourists. They are also symbols of the formal but tense relationship between the two countries that share 1,809 miles (2,911 km) of border.

Muslim Homeland

The name Pakistan comes from the **Persian** word *pak* for clean and pure, and the **Hindi** word *istan* for land. The country was designed as a homeland for Muslims of British India. Approximately 96 percent of Pakistanis are Muslim. The country is also home to small groups of **Hindus**, Christians, Sikhs, and people of other faiths whose ancestors lived in the lands of Pakistan for centuries.

- **OFFICIAL NAME:** The Islamic Republic of Pakistan
- **NATIONAL CAPITAL:** Islamabad
- **POPULATION:** 220.9 million
- **OFFICIAL LANGUAGES:** Urdu and English
- **LAND AREA:** 307,374 square miles (796,095 sq. km)

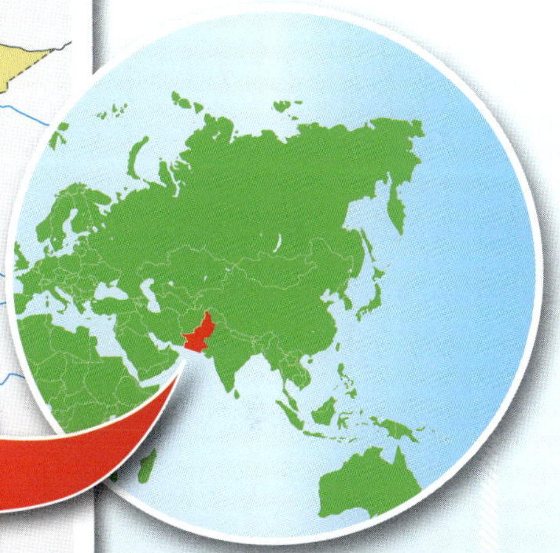

CHAPTER 1

The Land

Mountains, deserts, lush forests, fertile valleys, plateaus, and raging rivers—Pakistan's geography is stunning in its stark differences. Located in South Asia, the land of Pakistan stretches from the Arabian Sea in the southwest to the border of China in the east. Mountains, glaciers, and valleys mark the northern highlands, which include parts of the Hindu Kush, Karakoram, and Himalayan ranges.

The Indus River drains down through the country. This river and its **tributaries** were the home of some of the earliest human **civilizations** on Earth. People have lived there for at least 6,000 years, building cities and growing food on the river basins.

K2, the second-highest mountain in the world at 28,251 feet (8,611 m), reaches skyward in the Karakoram mountain range. It attracts climbers from all over the world to its dangerous peaks.

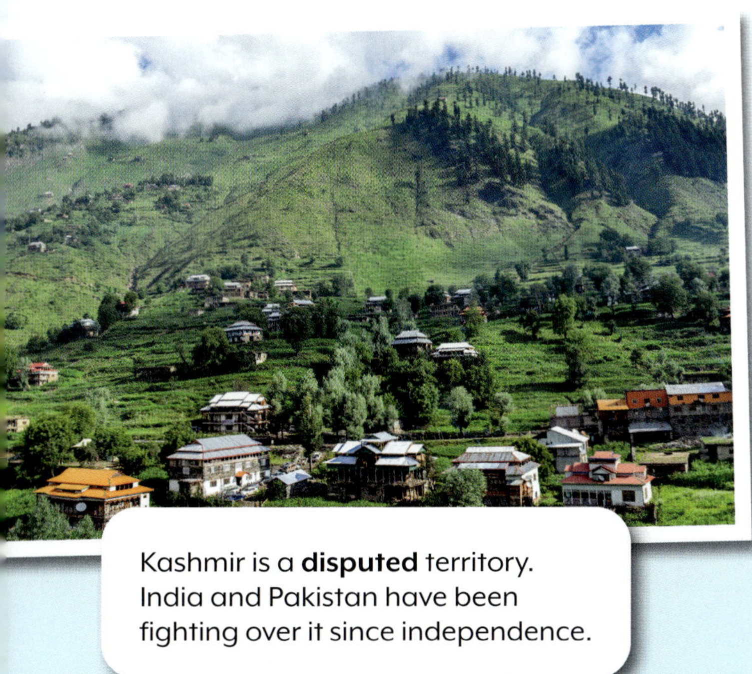

Kashmir is a **disputed** territory. India and Pakistan have been fighting over it since independence.

Provinces and Cities

Set amidst the beauty of Pakistan's varied landscapes are 10 sprawling cities with populations of several million and growing. There are hundreds more smaller cities, as well as villages spread out over four provinces: Sindh, Balochistan, Khyber Pakhtunkhwa, and Punjab. There are also two large autonomous, or self-governed, territories, Gilgit-Baltistan and Azad Kashmir, as well as the Islamabad Capital Territory. Pakistan has the fifth-largest population in the world, and it is growing. It is 33rd in the world in area, with many remote areas that are sometimes difficult to reach.

Mountains and Highlands

Pakistan's terrain is rugged and mountainous from the hilly southern area of Punjab province to the towering alpine peaks of northern Gilgit-Baltistan territory. There are 8,266 **named mountains** in Pakistan. Approximately 108 are above 22,966 feet (7,000 m) and another 4,555 are above 19,685 feet (6,000 m). These are some of the highest mountains in the world. Most of the highest are in the Karakoram range in Gilgit-Baltistan which borders China and India. K2, located there, is known as one of the most difficult mountains to climb and attracts mountain climbers from all over the world.

The Himalayan range also cuts through the north. Several other mountain ranges, such as the Pamir Mountains and the Hindu Kush, encircle the north and continue through the borders of neighboring Afghanistan and China. Many mountain villages grow crops such as wheat, barley, potatoes, and apricots in valleys that are between 9,842 to 10,827 feet (3,000 to 3,300 m) high. They also herd sheep, goats, and yaks in mountain pastures.

Rugged vehicles climb the steep mountain road to base camp at Nanga Parbat. This mountain, also known as Diamir, is called King of the Mountains because of its steep and dangerous peaks.

Yaks are related to cattle. They are kept and herded for their milk, meat, and pelts. They are mountain animals adapted to living at high elevations.

Many of Pakistan's glaciers "surge" instead of retreating with global warming.

Glaciers

Pakistan has more than 7,000 mountain glaciers—more than almost anywhere else on Earth. Only the polar regions have more. These glaciers supply rivers with **meltwater** in the summer. This water **engorges** rivers and helps **irrigate** crops and provide hydroelectric power. The 39-mile-long (62.7 km) Baltoro Glacier in Gilgit-Baltistan runs through the Karakoram mountain range. It is fed by other tributary glaciers.

Closer Look

Glacial Lake Outburst Flooding

In recent years, melting and shifting glaciers have become a threat to the people who live and farm in the mountains of Pakistan. Global warming has created outburst flooding. This is where the sudden release of meltwater from a glacier causes glacial lakes to flood or ice dams to burst. The water floods surrounding land, destroying houses, roads and bridges, power stations, orchards, and farmland.

Melting of the 7.5-mile-long (12 km) Shisper Glacier in Hunza, Gilgit-Baltistan, caused glacial outburst lake flooding in 2022. The flooding displaced 20 residents in the village of Hassanabad, crumbled the Hassanabad bridge, and damaged power stations.

Rivers of Life

Pakistan's rivers are the lifeblood of the country. They provide water for agriculture, drinking, and industry. The country's river system begins in the Himalayan and Karakoram mountains. Five of Pakistan's main rivers and their many tributaries flow south from the mountains into Punjab and Sindh provinces. The main rivers include the Jhelum, Chenab, Ravi, Beas, and Sultej, which all flow into the Indus. Many cities and villages are located on or near these rivers and tributaries.

The Gilgit River is another mountain tributary of the Indus that runs through Gilgit-Baltistan.

The Indus flows southwest 1,976 miles (3,180 km) through Pakistan and the disputed region of Kashmir.

The Indus

The Indus River is one of the longest rivers in the world. For thousands of years, it has supported life. Some of the world's earliest civilizations began on the banks of this mighty river. The Indus River is a snow and glacier-fed river that begins in Tibet. It meanders through gorges and by mountains and farming plains in several regions of Pakistan, before emptying into the Arabian Sea near the city of Karachi.

Indus River Plain

The Indus River plain is a broad area of fertile land that covers 200,000 square miles (518,000 sq. km). It slopes down from the mountains in the north to the Arabian Sea in the south. Many crops are grown along the plain, including corn, rice, wheat, **millet**, and further south, cotton and sugarcane.

Farmers plant rice in Lahore in the Indus River basin.

Balochistan Plateau

The Balochistan plateau lies on the northwest corner of Pakistan between Afghanistan and Iran. This is a tableland, or high plain, that lays east of the Sulaiman Mountains, which are part of the Hindu Kush and the Kirthar ranges. The Ziarat Juniper Forest is located there—the largest juniper forest in the country. This forest is a **biosphere reserve**. Its 27,782 acres (11,243 hectares) are protected from destruction, as human population growth is a threat to the unique plants and wildlife in the forest. Some of the trees there are 7,000 years old, or so old that they are considered living fossils. Wild pistachios and almonds also grow there. In the southeast is the Kharan Desert. A strip of coastal plain called Makran extends along the Gulf of Oman, where there are small fishing ports.

Gwadar is a fishing port on the coastal plain of Balochistan. Balochistan is also the name of Pakistan's largest province.

A herder guides his livestock through the hilly regions of the Balochistan plateau.

Deserts of Pakistan

About 10 percent of Pakistan's landmass is made up of deserts. These are areas of land that get less than 10 inches (25 cm) of precipitation per year. Pakistan's five deserts are located in different regions of the country. The Thar Desert in south Sindh province spans the border with India, where it is known as the Great Indian Desert. It is the world's 16th-largest desert, but only about 15 percent of it is in Pakistan. The Kharan Desert in Pakistan's southwestern Balochistan province covers 7,722 square miles (20,000 sq. km).

The Cholistan, or Rohi, Desert is in Punjab province. The city of Bahawalpur is located on the edge of the Cholistan. It was once part of a **princely state** that joined Pakistan in 1947. The Thal Desert is also located in Punjab province, between the Indus River and the Jhelum River.

Much of the 217-mile-long (350 km) Thal has been changed into farmland through a large canal and irrigation project. Irrigation allows green chickpeas and other crops to be grown there for half the year, while the other half of the year it returns to desert. The Katpana Desert is near the mountain village of Skardu in northern Gilgit-Baltistan territory. It is a cold desert with some sand dunes that are covered in snow during winter.

The Thar Desert is home to a number of Hindu people who have lived there for centuries.

The Derawar Fort is an old fort first built in the 800s in the Cholistan Desert.

The Khewra Salt Mine is the second largest in the world. Discovered more than 2,000 years ago, it has now become a major tourist attraction, with close to 250,000 visitors a year.

Natural Resources

One of Pakistan's enduring natural resources is its **arable** land. Roughly 28 percent of its land is cultivated. It is the world's fifth-largest producer of both sugarcane and mangoes. It also ranks sixth in date and seventh in wheat production. Pakistan is rich in minerals such as iron ore, coal, gold, and copper. One of the largest gold and copper mines is in Balochistan. Pakistan also has oil and gas reserves which continue to be developed. Limestone reserves support the cement industry. Rock salt, or the pink Himalayan salt used in cooking, is mined in the Salt Range mountains in Punjab province, south of the Himalayas.

Cats to Crocodiles

Varied climates and terrains mean Pakistan has a wide range of plant and animal life. More than 660 bird species and 177 mammals are known to exist in the country's deserts, plains, forests, and mountains. Some, like the Muree Hills frog, are only found in one specific area of Pakistan. The markhor, a large screw-horned wild goat, is the country's national animal. It lives in mountainous areas where it is skilled at climbing steep cliffs. Rare snow leopards, slender serval cats, fishing cats, cheetahs, and caracals are among the wild cats that live in Pakistan's varied landscapes. Mugger, or marsh, crocodiles, inhabit the rivers and marshes in the southwest.

Indus river dolphins, or bhulans, are toothed whales that live in the Indus. The dolphin's range and habitat have shrunk 80 percent since 1870, to only 429 miles (690 km) of the river. Water pollution and overfishing have made them a threatened species.

Closer Look

A Highway Runs Through It

The Karakoram Highway (KKH) is an 810-mile-long (1,300 km) national highway that meanders from Punjab province to the mountainous border of China at Khunjerab Pass. Sometimes called the "Eighth Wonder of the World," the KKH is one of the highest paved roads in the world. Parts of the highway trace the ancient Silk Road, a network of trade routes that brought silk and other desired goods from China to Central Asia and beyond. The KKH is a major trade route, and vehicles found driving on it include decorated "jingle trucks," as well as tour buses, cars, and even travelers on bicycles. Carved through three mountain ranges, the KKH was built jointly by Pakistan and China, from 1962 to 1978. More than 810 Pakistani and 200 Chinese road workers died from landslides and falls during the road's construction.

It takes skilled drivers to drive colorful Bedford "jingle trucks" on sections of the KKH where the road is narrow and landslides occur regularly.

The Karakoram Pass to China marks the highest point on the KKH, and the highest border crossing in the world.

Landslides are common on the KKH. A large section of the KKH was damaged by a landslide in 2010 that created Attabad Lake in northern Pakistan. For a time, trucks unloaded cargo onto boats that traveled the lake and unloaded on the other side of the highway. A new route around the lake was completed in 2015.

CHAPTER 2 Development

Many People, Many Cultures

Pakistan is both an ancient land and a relatively new state. Its many people and cultures represent a link with the past and present. Humans have lived in this area of South Asia since **Paleolithic** times. The Soan Valley, or Rawat area, in northern Punjab was believed to be home to *Homo erectus* groups who died out 117,000 to 108,000 years ago. These early humans were hunter-gatherers who used stone tools. The Mehrgarh site on the plains of Balochistan was uncovered in 1974. It dates back to 7000–5500 B.C.E. when humans were beginning to farm and build houses out of mud bricks. Modern archaeologists uncovering ancient human remains discovered that the earliest forms of dentistry were practiced there.

Many small Harappan toy models and figurines have been discovered in the remains of the Indus Valley villages.

Harappan cities were noted for their planning, drainage and water supply systems, and the use of baked bricks.

A seal found at the Mohenjo-daro site shows what is believed to be a deity, possibly the Hindu god Shiva, Lord of the Animals.

Indus Valley Civilization

The Indus Valley Civilization is one of the most well-known ancient civilizations. It covered areas in the basin of the Indus River and its tributaries from 3300 B.C.E. until about 1700 B.C.E. The remains of Indus Valley villages can be found in Sindh, Punjab, and Balochistan. The people who lived in these villages were called the Harappans. They were known for building cities that had 5,000 or more people. There, the Harappans built multistory houses and early sewage systems.

The Mohenjo-daro archaeological site in Sindh is one of the largest settlements of the Indus Valley Civilization. It was built around 2500 B.C.E. and is considered one of the earliest planned cities in the world. Archaeologists have uncovered public baths, a granary, large assembly halls, and wells.

Mohenjo-daro was one of the world's earliest cities. Today, its remains have been designated a **UNESCO World Heritage site**.

Many Empires, Many Rulers

Ancient Pakistan was a melting pot of many cultures and rulers. Its location at the crossroads of East, South, and Central Asia has meant people from all of these areas **migrated** to its fertile lands. Over thousands of years, dozens of kingdoms, empires, dynasties, and **caliphates** have ruled. Each one left its mark.

Vedic Period

After the Indus Valley Civilization collapsed around 1900 B.C.E., groups of Indo-Aryan peoples migrated to the area from Central Asia. They brought their religious practices with them. Their beliefs were written in an ancient language called Vedic Sanskrit. These became the Rigveda, the hymns of life and gods that are part of the Hindu belief system today. The Indo-Aryan peoples established several kingdoms in different areas of what is now modern Pakistan and India. Their rule was called the Vedic Period, and lasted from 1500 to 500 B.C.E.

An ancient Buddha statue from the Kushan Empire, Gandhara, Pakistan. The Kushan Empire was a northern Chinese empire that ruled parts of Pakistan in the 1st century C.E.

Alexander the Great and his army conquered the Achaemenid Empire and launched a campaign to gain control of its territory in Pakistan in 327 B.C.E.

Prized Territory

Almost every major ancient Indo-European and Asian empire ruled over parts of Pakistan. Its lands and people were once part of the Achaemenid Empire, an enormous ancient Persian empire founded by Cyrus the Great in 550 B.C.E. Later, Alexander the Great brought his army through northern Pakistan and made it part of the Macedonian Empire. Most of Pakistan came under the ancient Indian Mauryan Empire in 325 B.C.E.

Religions and Cultures

Other kingdoms and empires of Greek, Central Asian, Iranian, northern Chinese, Indian, and **Mongol** origin followed. Each conquest and invasion brought new cultures, languages, and religions to the lands of Pakistan. Some people followed Hindu beliefs, some followed Buddhist, and many had ancient **animist** beliefs. In 712 C.E., most of the Indus region was conquered by the Umayyad Empire, a Muslim caliphate from the Middle East. The caliphate brought Islam to Pakistan, which spread over time and with later Muslim dynasties.

The Dharmarajika Stupa near the ancient Taxila site in Pakistan dates from the 2nd century C.E. Taxila is a Sanskrit word that means "city of cut stone." Taxila was an ancient city founded around 550 B.C.E. during the Achaemenid Empire. It was a center of learning that survived through several other empires.

Mughal Empire

The Muslim-led Mughal Empire was one of the wealthiest and most powerful in the world from 1526–1857. Over time, the Mughals lost their empire and were replaced by other rulers and empires, including the British, who ruled before Pakistan's independence.

The first Mughal ruler was Babur who founded a dynasty that continued through 19 emperors who eventually ruled over 150 million people.

The British in Pakistan

England, and later Britain, took an interest in the wealth and territory of the rulers of Pakistan and India beginning in the 1600s. Through the **East India Company**, it waged wars and gained a **monopoly** on trade and territory. This lasted for more than 200 years. Over time, the **British crown** took over and ruled directly. This was known as the British Raj. The Raj made the lands of Pakistan and India part of the British Empire. A growing number of people in India rejected British rule and the idea that they were just one people instead of many. Over many years, they held protests, strikes, and **mutinies** to press for independence. The rule of the Raj lasted until 1947 when Pakistan and India gained independence.

Lahore Fort in the Walled City of Lahore was built by Mughal emperors.

Closer Look

Partition sparked one of the greatest migrations of humans in history. Fifteen million people became refugees. They moved on foot or by train.

Muhammad Ali Jinnah was a lawyer and politician who fought for an independent Pakistan. Known as Pakistan's "Father of the Nation," he became the country's first governor-general in 1947, but died a year later. His birthday is a national holiday known as Quaid-e-Azam Day, or "Great Leader" Day.

Partition and Loss of East Pakistan

Partition divided Pakistan and India into two countries. It split land and people along religious lines. Pakistan became a Muslim-majority country. India became a Hindu-majority country. There were violent clashes and **massacres** as millions of people left Pakistan for India and India for Pakistan. An estimated 2 million people were killed. Border disputes between Pakistan and India continue to this day. But that wasn't Pakistan's only early trauma. The country was separated into two geographically distant parts: East Pakistan and West Pakistan. West Pakistan was larger and more populous. The people there were different culturally and spoke a different language. When Urdu was chosen as Pakistan's official language, it led to clashes and eventually a war of liberation for the east. East Pakistan declared independence in 1971 and became the country of Bangladesh.

CHAPTER 3

Life Today

Children carry sand from the bank of the Ravi River in Lahore to sell to brick factories.

Children spend their days working at a brick factory. Bricks are made by mixing soil and water. They are then placed in a brick mold that is baked in a kiln.

Pakistan's population boomed in the decades after partition, expanding from almost 34 million in 1951 to 220 million in 2021. It now has the third-highest population growth rate in the world. The country's population is expected to hit 403 million by the year 2050. Much of the population is young, with 64 percent under the age of 30. This kind of growth has had an impact on the country, its economy, government, and future. Pakistan's economy is the 24th largest in the world.

Weathy and Poor

Average incomes are lower than many other countries and there is a wide gap between the wealthy and the poor. The wealthiest people have almost five times the income of the poorest. Just 20 percent of the population accounts for half of the total income generated in the country. Much of the wealth comes from land ownership. In many rural areas, people rent their land and work as sharecroppers who give a part of their crop as rent. If they have large families, it may mean it is difficult to feed, clothe, and send all of their children to school. Some children may be forced to work to support their families. Some provinces have laws banning children under the age of 14 from working. Still, organizations such as UNICEF suggest between 3.3 million and 12.5 million children in Pakistan ages 10–14 are working and not attending school.

A boy fixes and paints shoes for a living in Karachi.

Wealthy Pakistanis gather at a wedding.

Growth and the Environment

One of Pakistan's greatest challenges in the future will be keeping up with growth and protecting the environment. A growing population will put strain on a country already stressed by extreme temperatures and rapid deforestation. Summer temperatures can soar to 100 °F (37.7 °C) in Punjab. Temperatures have been increasing in recent years. Pakistan has been pegged as the eighth country most affected by climate change. While not a big emitter of greenhouse gases that trap heat, it experiences worldwide climate change brought on by more developed and industrialized countries in North America and Europe. Melting glaciers have created outburst flooding in Pakistan's mountainous regions. Heavier than normal monsoon rains in summer 2022 created deadly floods throughout one-third of the country. About 33 million people were affected. Many lost homes and livelihoods. An estimated 1,300 people were killed and 1,300 were injured.

Women wade through waist-deep floodwater in the city of Hyderabad, Sindh province. Experts believe Pakistan will continue to be battered by climate change-related floods and droughts.

Farm workers use a rice thresher to separate rice from grass stocks at a farm in Larkana, Sindh province.

Farming and Food Industry

Roughly 1 percent of Pakistan's farmers own 22 percent of its agricultural land. Yet farming employs about 43 percent of the workforce. In many parts of the country, this land has been passed down from generation to generation by a few families. Large landowners grow crops such as sugarcane, mango, cotton, rice, and wheat for domestic consumption and export. Some rent land to small farmers. Others own commercial farms and employ people to farm and raise livestock for market. Cattle, water buffaloes, sheep, goats, and camels are farmed for milk and meat. Pakistan is the fourth-largest producer of milk in the world. Much of Pakistan's crops are processed within the country, making food and beverage processing the second-largest industry in the country. It is also a growing industry.

Water buffaloes are milked at a commercial farm.

A yak rests after grazing on communal pasture in the Pamir mountains. One of SNT's objectives is to build programs by and for women of Shimshal. In Shimshal, unlike other communities, women are traditionally the summer herders in the high pastures.

Shimshal Nature Trust and Land Protection

In some areas of Pakistan, yaks, goats, and sheep are raised on communally owned pastures. This means everyone in a community shares and looks after the land where their animals graze. This traditional way of grazing has made many communities protective of the land and environment. When the government of Pakistan established Khunjerab National Park to protect mountain wildlife, it tried to control the traditional pastureland of the village of Shimshal, in the Karakoram mountains of Gilgit-Baltistan. Shimshalis had always **sustainably** managed and farmed the area and refused to give up their traditional grazing rights. The village established the Shimshal Nature Trust (SNT) in 1997 as a community-based conservation organization.

Shimshal's relationship to its mountain environment is expressed in its culture. The **Wakhi**-speaking people who live there understand how to care for and preserve the environment. The SNT was formed to protect the rights of the people of Shimshal and the lands in their territory. It also develops programs to train nature stewards, protect mountain culture, and establish a mountaineering school and visitors program. In 2008, SNT received a Science and Practice of Ecology & Society Award. SNT even partnered with the government in 2020 on a Protected Areas Initiative to train young villagers to act as custodians and guards for Kunjerab National Park. This protects nature and grazing rights, and provides jobs.

Major Industries

Check the back of your shirt. It may say "Made in Pakistan." If not, maybe the fabric was made in Pakistan or the raw cotton was sourced from Pakistan. Cotton farming and textile production employs about 40 percent of the country's industrial workers and supports 10 million farmers. The industry is growing, but one barrier to growth is regular power outages in the country's cities. These are caused by poor electricity **infrastructure**. Power blackouts can mean work is stopped in factories for hours or days at a time. Leather goods are another major Pakistani export industry. There are more than 800 tanneries in the country making cow, sheep, buffalo, and goat skin for the leather goods industry.

Automotive, Chemical, and Mining

The automotive, chemical, and mining industries are also growing in Pakistan. Pakistan's auto industry produces 1.8 million motorcycles and over 200,000 vehicles as well as parts each year. It is one of the fastest-growing automotive industries in Asia. Several major auto manufacturers have plants in Pakistan. The country's chemical industry produces paint, plastics, detergents, dyes, and paper, as well as perfumes. Pakistan is also a center for mining of precious and semi-precious stones and minerals. It has been known for its rubies and emeralds since ancient times. Today, these as well as peridot, aquamarine, topaz, and quartz are mined in Khyber Pakhtunkhwa and Balochistan. Coal deposits are mined in Sindh.

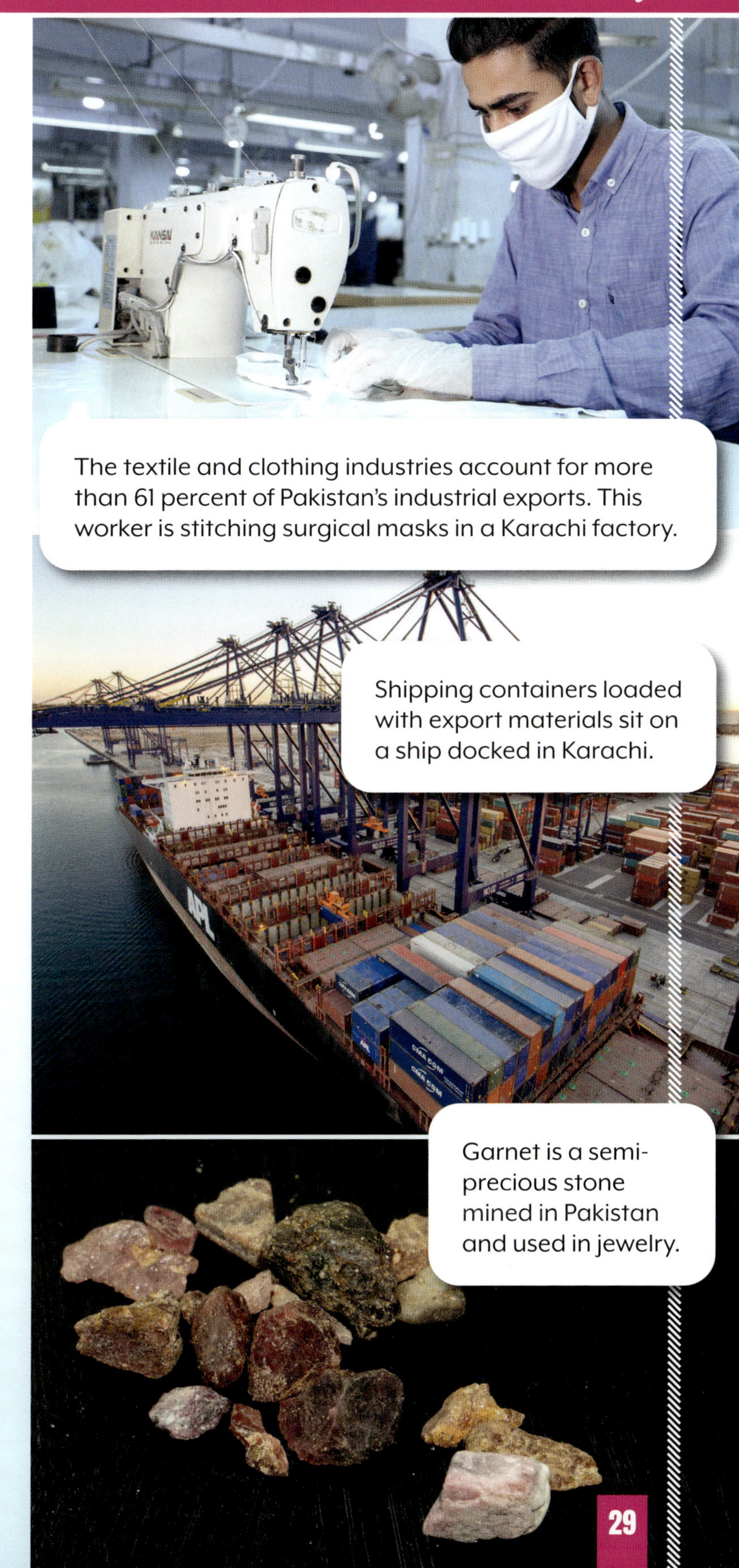

The textile and clothing industries account for more than 61 percent of Pakistan's industrial exports. This worker is stitching surgical masks in a Karachi factory.

Shipping containers loaded with export materials sit on a ship docked in Karachi.

Garnet is a semi-precious stone mined in Pakistan and used in jewelry.

Going to School

Pakistan's **constitution** guarantees free state education to children between the ages of five and 16. Many state schools are not well funded, and teachers are poorly paid. In rural areas in provinces such as Balochistan, schools may be located great distances from villages. It can be hard for children to attend. Some Pakistani parents choose to send their children to private schools that they pay for themselves. Boys and girls often attend separate schools. Because of poverty and **gender inequality**, many children don't go to school regularly, or at all. Approximately 22.7 million children do not attend school. Girls from poorer families are least likely to be sent to school. Only 41 percent of girls attend school by grade 6.

About 32,000 madrassas, or religious schools, provide free religious education throughout Pakistan. Both boys and girls can attend from age five. They memorize the Quran, or Muslim holy book, and learn Arabic, math, and other subjects. About 2.5 million children and youths attend madrassas.

These girls in Skardu, Gilgit-Baltistan, attend a village school.

Pakistan has 7,383 miles (11,881 km) of train tracks. Most are up to 100 years old. Many main lines, like the one that runs from Karachi to Lahore, are being upgraded. New ones are proposed.

Transit systems within cities are privately owned. People take buses or use auto rickshaws called tuk tuks.

Traveling Through

Vast terrain that is difficult to navigate characterizes much of Pakistan. Yet some of the most well-known ancient roads and trade routes cut through much of Pakistan. The Grand Trunk Road was one of South Asia's oldest roads. Its northern parts ran through Lahore and Rawalpindi to Peshawar for more than 2,000 years. The modern Karakoram Highway (KKH) echoes some of the southern parts of the ancient Silk Road from China. The KKH is part of a network of national highways of Pakistan that covers 7,537 miles (12,131 km.) They include the modernized Grand Trunk Road, the Indus Highway, and the Makran Coastal Highway. Each links major regions of the country. Other regional motorways linking to them were built within the past few decades. Pakistan is part of China's Belt and Road Initiative (BRI) that will build a modern Silk Road through Pakistan, Central Asia, Europe, and Africa. A 684-mile-long (1,100 km) motorway is planned from Karachi to Islamabad and then through the KKH to the Chinese border.

This modern road follows part of the old Grand Trunk Road in Parachinar, Pakistan.

CHAPTER 4

A Vibrant Country

"As-Salaam-Alaikum" is what Pakistanis say when they greet people. It means "peace be upon you" in Arabic. Many respond to this with "Wa-Alaikum-Salaam," which means "and peace unto you." This common greeting is used in a country where most people are Muslim and where more than 70 languages are spoken. Some Pakistanis will also place their right hand over their heart when addressing loved ones and strangers alike.

Pakistan is a modern country where people have strong connections to the past and traditions. There are 15 major ethnic groups and hundreds of smaller ones. Each group may have a different mother tongue, history, customs, and often, way of life. Pakistanis are united by family and community bonds and at the state level, an official language—Urdu. Urdu is a language native to South Asia and is similar to Hindi, the official language of India. Urdu and English were chosen as Pakistan's two official languages in 1947.

Street signs are often written in English and Urdu script. English is the language of the British colonizers who ruled British India before partition.

Urdu and chai tea are two common elements in Pakistan. Urdu is spoken throughout the country, and everybody drinks chai. Here chai is served by a street chai wallah in Karachi.

Many Languages

Urdu is taught in schools and used in government. People speak it interchangeably with English and other regional languages of Pakistan. Many Pakistanis speak at least three or four languages. Other widely used languages include Punjabi, which is also spoken in India. Punjabi people are the largest ethnic group in Pakistan, making up over 44 percent of the population. Within the group, there are many different "tribes," or groups.

Pashto is another major language, spoken by 15 percent of Pakistanis. Pashto is an Iranian language of the Pashtun or Pathan people, an ethnic group who originate from Afghanistan. There are hundreds of different Pashtun tribes or clans. Sindhi and Saraiki are commonly spoken languages in southern Pakistan. Sindhi is the mother tongue of almost 15 percent of Pakistanis, many in Sindh province. There are more than 25 million Saraiki speakers in Pakistan, many of them in Punjab and Sindh.

A Pashtun shoe cobbler waits for customers at his shoe repair shop. There are 26 million Pashtuns in Pakistan, and 11 million in neighboring Afghanistan. Human rights activist Malala Yousafzai is a famous Pakistani Pashtun.

A Sindhi village grandmother prepares vegetables for a meal.

A Pashto film poster outside of an old Karachi theater.

State Religion

Pakistan's culture is shaped by Islam, the main religion, as much as it is influenced by geography and **ethnicity**. The country's social values reflect all of these. About 85 to 90 percent of Pakistanis are Sunni Muslims and 10 to 15 percent are Shia. Islam is also the state religion of Pakistan and this is reflected in its politics and some laws. Mosques, or masjids, are places of prayer in Islam. Pakistan has thousands of mosques. Many are beautiful and historically important. The Badshahi Mosque in Lahore was built in 1673 for the Mughal emperor Aurangzeb. The Faisal Mosque in Islamabad is the largest mosque in South Asia and one of the biggest in the world. This modern mosque was designed to look like a desert tent and was completed in 1986.

Ismaili Muslims are Shia Muslims, whose leader, or imam, is the Aga Khan. Instead of mosques, they gather in jamatkhanas. The Kharadar Jamatkhana in Karachi was built in the 1800s.

The Wazir Khan Mosque in Lahore is known for its detailed interior tile work.

The Kalash people celebrate festivals that honor their gods and protect their herds. The festivals often attract tourists and provide another form of income for the Kalash.

The Kalash People

The Kalash are an ethnic minority and **Indigenous** people who live in the Hindu Kush mountains of Khyber Pakhtunkhwa. They are non-Muslim farmers and herders who follow an ancient animist belief system. The Kalash language is Indo-European and researchers say their ancestors came to the mountains about 12,000 years ago from Northern and Western Asia. Some Kalash stories claim they are the **descendants** of Alexander the Great's army. There is no genetic evidence of this. Their language and culture is like no other in Pakistan. Although some have **converted** to Islam over the last century, most still follow their ancient traditions.

Closer Look

The Shalwar Kameez

Not many countries have a **national dress** that can be formal or informal, **unisex**, and worn for almost everything. Pakistan's national dress—the shalwar kameez—is a versatile set of clothing worn by many people in their daily lives. Shalwars are trousers, or pants, usually with a string-pulled waist called a nala. Kameez are long, tunic-style shirts. Worn together, they suit all weather and occasions and are comfortable and cool in warm climates. Shalwar kameez also fit Islamic dress requirements that men and women stay covered and modest. Pakistanis wear Western-style clothing as well, but the shalwar kameez is worn everywhere in the country, often with regional style variations. Women also wear a long scarf called a dupatta draped around the neck. Dupattas can be easily pulled over the head and shoulders for modesty when out in public.

Shopkeepers in Peshawar wear shalwar kameez. A young girl wears a shalwar kameez with a dupatta over her head and neck.

Festivals and Celebrations

Pakistanis love a get-together with family and friends. Religious and national holidays and community celebrations often include a lot of food, games, chatting, and music. Many Muslim religious holidays are national holidays and major events. Ramadan, the ninth month of the Islamic calendar, is widely observed. People fast during the day and attend mosque. Eid al-Fitr and Eid al-Adha are two major religious celebrations. They include large feasts, where people wear and give new clothing. They also give gifts to children and the poor. Muharram is a month of solemn remembrance and meditation for Shia Muslims. It is often marked alongside Ashura where the death of the grandson of Muhammad is mourned.

Chilam Joshi Festival, Chitral

Pakistanis also celebrate non-religious holidays that mark the seasons. Rural or farming areas have spring planting or fall harvest festivals. These include feasts with special foods, and sports events such as tug-of-war contests. Other celebrations commemorate historic events or significant dates. Almost everyone marks Independence Day on August 14.

Basant is a spring festival where people traditionally take part in kite-flying competitions.

Men gather for Friday prayers during the holy month of Ramadan in Peshawar.

Closer Look

Shandur Polo Festival

Polo is one of the oldest sports in the world. It is a passion in Pakistan's north, where people claim it originated. The world's highest polo grounds, the Shandur Pass in the mountains of Khyber Pakhtunkhwa, are also home to an annual polo festival. Every July, polo teams from Gilgit-Baltistan compete with Chitral. This wild, freestyle, no-rules match at an elevation of 12,139 feet (3,700 m) is fast and sometimes frightening. Riders don't wear helmets, and horses sometimes collapse and are carried off the field. People come from all over Pakistan to watch the match.

A polo player from the city of Gilgit in Gilgit-Baltistan chases down a polo ball.

Foods and Feasts

Hospitality is an important part of the Pakistani way of life. Guests are considered a blessing and serving them food and drink is important. Pakistani food is regional and has its roots in the many ethnic cultures that live in the country. Sindhis may eat more spicy foods, while Pashtuns eat more meat and kebabs. The Kalash are known for their breads made from nut flours, while people in Hunza in Gilgit-Baltistan eat a soup made from apricots. Karahis, or curries, are popular in Punjab as well as all over the country, and are served with flatbreads called naan, or chapatis. Pulaos and biryanis are mixed rice, meat, and vegetable dishes with Persian roots. Chaat is a spicy vegetable or fruit dish served by the Mughal emperors. Throughout the country, Muslims follow Islamic dietary laws in which foods are halal, or permissible to eat. Utensils such as forks are not commonly used for many meals. Instead, people eat with their right hand.

A street vendor in Lahore serves up samosas.

Spice wallahs sell spices and karahi mixtures in bazaars.

A couple signs a marriage contract during a wedding ceremony in Karachi. An Islamic marriage contract outlines the bride and groom's rights and obligations.

Weddings and Families

Pakistanis are connected through family and relationships. People look to their own family, relatives, and friends for support instead of the government. In this way, marriages are unions between other families. Traditionally, many marriages in Pakistan were and still are "arranged marriages." In these, parents look for suitable partners for their children and arrange the marriage like a business deal. More recently, couples are choosing semi-arranged marriages, where they are introduced to potential partners through family. Some couples are "love matches" who may meet their partners at school or through friends.

Weddings are special events. The ceremonies might be small, but the celebrations and receptions are a big deal. They can mean at least three days of rituals and traditions, singing, and eating. There are also several clothing changes for brides and grooms. Brides have elaborate mehndi designs made with **henna** painted on their hands. For the ceremony, called a barat, they wear red. Brides are given many sets of wedding jewelry. These are considered part of their wealth.

Brides have mehndi patterns stained on their hands with henna dye during mehndi parties prior to their weddings.

Sounds of the Country

The music of Pakistan is as diverse as its population. Wander through a bazaar and you'll hear shops playing Western-style pop or rap music in Urdu, upbeat Punjabi bhangra, traditional ghazals, and Urdu film music. The sound of a beautiful azzan, or Muslim call to prayer, might be carried on the wind from a nearby mosque. Some Pakistani music is deeply spiritual and religious. Qawwali is the devotional music of Sufis. Many qawwali singers train their entire lives. They are backed by eight to 10 musicians and other singers called a "party." Qawwali concerts can go on for many hours.

In "up country," or northern and eastern regions of Pakistan, folk musicians play instruments such as the rabab. This large stringed instrument is like a lute and has its origins in Central Asia.

Ghazals are long poems of love, loss, and devotion performed by singers trained in classical South Asian music. Noor Jehan was a famous ghazal singer who also acted in many Indian and Pakistani films. Abida Parveen is a composer and singer of both ghazals and qawwali, as well as other Sufi music.

The beat of the dohl, or double-headed drum, accompanies these Bhangra dancers. Bhangra is a form of dance and music that originated in Punjab.

Film and Dance

Pakistanis love a good movie, especially when it's a musical—and almost all Pakistani movies are musicals. In Pakistan, the film industry is centered around Karachi and Lahore, or "Lollywood." Lollywood is a combination of Lahore, where most Pakistani films were made until recently, and Hollywood. Lollywood movies are made in Urdu, Punjabi, Pashto, and Sindhi. Most are musicals that feature dancing as well.

Atiqa Odho is a famous Pakistani television and film actress.

Dancers perform at the Lahore Literary Festival. The festival celebrates the written word and how it relates to literature, film, television, and journalism.

CHAPTER 5 Looking to the Future

Pakistan stands out as a complex country. It is both ancient and new, as well as traditional and modern. It is home to people from many ethnic and cultural backgrounds and faiths. It is an Islamic republic—the largest of only three in the world.

Pakistan is also a democracy that struggled with maintaining justice and freedoms for its people after partition. Its history as a country includes four wars, corruption, attempted overthrows of the government, and periods of **martial law**. Continuous stable government is one key to Pakistan's future. Another is managing population growth. Growing population threatens food, water, and energy security. Pakistan's One Nation One Vision plan for 2025 is a government plan for a sustainable future. It includes improving education and literacy rates and building more schools. It also includes reforms to government, police, justice, and tax systems with the goal of curbing corruption.

Pakistan Navy commandos display their anti-terrorism skills during Defence Day celebrations on September 6. Pakistan's military is a powerful force within the country, and the sixth-largest military in the world, which accounts for a lot of the country's budget.

Despite its developing nation status, for over 40 years Pakistan has offered safety from war and terrorism for more than 4 million refugees from Afghanistan. About 1.4 million registered Afghans remain in Pakistan, working and attending school.

Pakistan's capital city, Islamabad, was built as a "planned city" to be modern but still Islamic. It has planned parks and roads.

Growing Pains

There has been much change and modernization in the years since partition and independence in 1947. An entirely new city—Islamabad—was built as the capital. But Pakistan faces many challenges. Its infrastructure of roads, bridges, hospitals, and modern education systems require improvements. As a developing economy, Pakistan relies on foreign aid and partnerships with non-governmental organizations to make many of these improvements. Tax reforms could direct more money to these projects. The gap between the wealthy and the poor is large. Improving education and education funding is one way to reduce income inequality.

Karachi (shown here) and Lahore are Pakistan's "mega cities." They developed without formal planning. In some areas, 400 people live on a single acre. Pakistan is just now developing planning and mapping strategies for these cities that include pedestrian-friendly walking areas.

Hot and Hotter

Global warming is already affecting Pakistan, with hotter and more deadly heat waves. Rapidly melting glaciers have already destroyed farmland, homes, bridges, and roads. Pakistan's Climate Action Plan includes nature-based solutions such as planting massive amounts of trees, and forest conservation programs. As an already low carbon-emitting nation, Pakistan has committed to reduce 50 percent of its harmful emissions by 2030 by changing from fossil fuel energy to renewable energy. It may not get there as it relies on funding from high-emitting countries to implement its plans. The government's One Nation One Vision plan lists Pakistan's untapped coal reserves as a fuel source by developing clean coal-burning technologies.

A woman carries firewood to her home in a Hunza village. Some Pakistanis heat their homes and cook with firewood.

Nuclear and Solar Power

Almost one-third of Pakistan's population does not have any form of electric power. Expanding and improving access to power, while simultaneously working on energy conservation, requires new methods. These include building new nuclear power plants and using more solar and wind power.

The Mangla Dam hydro power plant on the Jhelum River in Azad Jammu and Kashmir (AJK) was built in the 1960s. With the help of a $150 million grant from the United States in 2012, it was expanded.

Pakistan is the world's fourth most polluted country. Pollution from carbon emissions from vehicle exhaust, field burning, and tire burning creates smog like this in Lahore. Pakistan is making slow progress on air pollution **mitigation** plans, including tree planting.

A doctor checks the health of a boy at a medical clinic in Multan.

Food and Water Security

One in three Pakistanis do not have enough nutritious food to eat. Malnutrition results in stunted growth in children. Improving crop yields and agricultural methods is another goal of the One Nation One Vision plan. The aim is to reduce the food-insecure population from 60 percent to 30 percent.

Global warming and poor water management have moved Pakistan from a water-stressed country to a water-scarce country. Water scarcity means the supply of clean water is not adequate for agriculture, industry, or human use. Pakistan is working to change this by improving water storage for rain and surface water.

animist The belief that objects, places, and creatures possess a spiritual essence

arable Able to produce crops

bazaar A market with rows of shops selling goods, clothing, and food items

biosphere reserve Sites that are recognized by the United Nations Educational, Scientific and Cultural Organization (UNESCO) as places where people are trying to live in harmony with their environment. They are used for testing different forms of sustainable development.

British crown The monarchy, or kings and queens, of Britain and the United Kingdom

British India The direct rule of the British Crown on the Indian subcontinent, also called the British Raj

caliphate The rule of a caliph, or chief Muslim ruler

civilization An advanced stage of human culture and development

colony A country or area under partial or full control of another, more distant country

constitution The basic principles and laws by which a country is governed

converted Changed from one religion or belief to another

densely Crowded or closely compacted

descendant Someone who is related to a person or group of people who lived in the past

disputed Something that is argued or fought about

diverse Something that shows a great variety

East India Company An English merchant trading company that was formed in 1600 to trade in the Indian Ocean region and later East and South Asia

engorge To swell with liquid

ethnicity Belonging to a specific or several specific social, racial, or cultural groups

fragant A sweet, tasty, or pleasant smell

gender inequality The act of not treating people equally based on their gender

henna The powdered leaves of a tropical shrub used to dye hair or decorate the body

Hindi A language of northern India that is now the fourth most widely spoken language in the world

Hindu A follower of Hinduism, a major South Asian religious and cultural tradition

Indigenous Native to a particular place. Indigenous peoples are the original inhabitants of a place.

infrastructure The equipment or structures, such as roads and water supply, that a country or region needs to function properly

irrigate To supply land with water so that crops and plants will grow

martial law Rule by military government

massacre The violent killing of many people

medieval Dating to or relating to the Middle Ages, a period of time from about 500 to 1500 C.E.

meltwater Water flowing from melting glaciers and ice

migrated Moved from one country or place to live in another

millet A cereal plant that grows fast and in poor soil and that is harvested for flour

minarets Towers built into or near mosques and often used to announce a call to prayer

mitigation The act of making something less severe or harmful

Mongol An East Asian ethnic group native to Mongolia and the Mongol Empire from the 1200s to the late 1300s

monopoly Complete control of a service or supply of goods

Mughal Member of a Muslim dynasty that ruled the lands of Pakistan and India from the 1500s to the 1800s

mutinies Open rebellions against an authority

named mountains Mountains that have been named after something or someone

national dress The clothing worn or chosen as representing the culture of a country

Paleolithic Relating to the early part of the Stone Age, roughly 2.5 million years to 10,000 B.C.E.

Persian Native to, or coming from Persia, now the country of Iran

princely state In British India, states or areas that had an Indian ruler but one that did not have full power

resource Something that a country possesses that it can use to increase its wealth

shalwar kameez South Asian clothing consisting of a long shirt called a kameez worn with trousers or pants

sustainably Something made, established, or grown in a way that it can survive in the future

tributaries Rivers or streams that flow into larger rivers or lakes

tuk tuks Three-wheeled motorized vehicles used as taxis

UNESCO World Heritage site A protected landmark or area singled out by the United Nations Educational, Scientific, and Cultural Organization as being globally significant

unisex Designed for both men and women

Wakhi The language of the Wakhi people, an Iranian ethnic group native to Central and South Asia

Books

Bedell, Jane Marie. *Teens in Pakistan.* Compass Point Books, 2009.

Razzak, Shazia. *P is for Pakistan.* Frances Lincoln Children's Books, 2007.

Wagner, Heather Lehr. *India and Pakistan.* Chelsea House, 2002.

Websites

Learn facts about Pakistan:
https://kids.britannica.com/kids/article/Pakistan/345761

Find out more details about Pakistan:
www.cia.gov/the-world-factbook/countries/pakistan

Explore Pakistan's culture from an insider's perspective:
https://culturalatlas.sbs.com.au/pakistani-culture/pakistani-culture-core-concepts

About the Author

Ellen Rodger has written more than 50 books for kids and youths on topics as varied as narwhals, Fetal Alcohol Spectrum Disorder, and potatoes. She spent some time traveling and hiking in Pakistan and counts Nusrat Fateh Ali Khan as one of her favorite musical artists.